THIS WORKBOOK

. ᴝ

IF FOUND
PLEASE CONTACT

A BRIEF INTRODUCTION TO
STENCIL TYPE

STENCILS HAVE BEEN EMPLOYED BY ARTISTS AND CRAFTS-people for centuries. As a technique for quickly and inexpensively reproducing shapes and images, the stencil is an unparalleled tool. It's very easy to see the connection that stencils have to letterforms. Stencil letters are widely available in commercial hardware stores, allowing anyone to make concise, readable forms at a larger scale. Stencils can serve as a guide for clear and efficient lettering, freeing the user from the technicalities of handwriting, which can often be inconsistent, highly personal, and subjective in its communication. Besides their utilitarian use, stencil letters have come to signify a scrappy D I Y aesthetic sensibility.

STENCILETTER is built on a simple premise: by deconstructing letters into simpler shapes, users are free to explore an infinite number of combinations to create letterforms. The work of two designers in particular, W. A. Dwiggins (1880–1956) and Joan Trochut (1920–80), exemplifies the range of expression that simple, repeated geometric shapes can serve in the creation of letterforms. Dwiggins employed stencils heavily in the creation of his illustrations, lettering designs, and typeface designs. He understood that the foundation of the alphabet lies in the repetition of shapes, and that deconstructing and rearranging these shapes could yield new designs, new forms, and new means for graphic communication. Trochut, meanwhile, focused his energy on making a modular shape–based toolset available to letterpress printers such as Super Tipo Veloz. This allowed printers to offer their customers unique designs.

Included in this STENCILETTER kit are four stencils: two stencils of purely geometric shapes, a stencil of ornamental shapes, and another stencil of a full, premade alphabet of characters. We hope you enjoy playing with STENCILETTER and encourage you to use these stencils as a way to explore the endless creative possibilities within a modest framework!

—CHARLES & THORN

STENCILETTER

STENCILETTER is a powerful, all-in-one kit for making letters, illustrations, and compositions. Fortunately, there is no real secret to using this kit: just pick it up and play! Below are a few pointers to get you started:

1 Pick a theme for your letters! Are the letters made entirely of circles or squares? Are they a mixture of both? Try using a theme to generate an entire alphabet of letters.

2 New paths are often discovered by retracing the steps of others! If you don't feel comfortable improvising from the get-go, try recreating the provided letter styles, and see where it leads you.

3 There is no wrong way to play! The more fun you have with these stencils, the more likely you are to stumble on a unique creation! Try using different colors, writing tools, and materials.

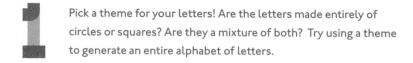

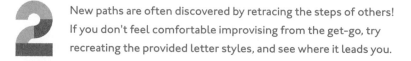

Think big! Use multiple shapes together to build giant letters.

Color pencils and color fine-tip markers are ideal to work with. Avoid broad-tipped markers or other writing tools that bleed heavily.

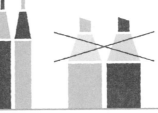

Overlay two stencils for even more possibilities with masking effects!

No need to fill every shape! Experiment with shading, outlining, and patterning of shapes.

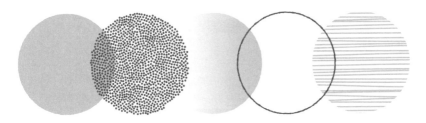

ABCDEF
GHIJKL
MNOPQ
RSTUWX
Y&Z

— TRY THIS —
Try making a monolinear
letter set using only the
thin lines and curves.

Aa Bb Dd

Ee Ff Gg Hh

hi jk Lm no p

Rr Ss Tu

uv w x y z

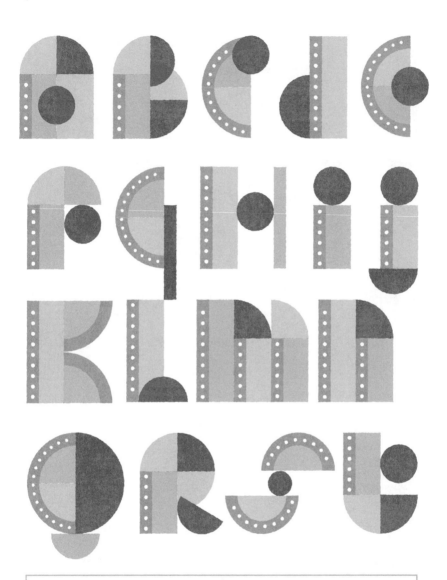

— ALL IN THE DETAILS —

Try using a white pen or thin marker to overlay detail lines on top of your design! Use the detailed stencil, or make up your own.

ABCDEF
GHIJKL
MNOPQ
RST

— WHY NOT? —

Make an abstract and super-geometric alphabet! Push yourself to see how abstracted you can make your letters while keeping them legible and readable. You'll be surprised at how wild they can get!